THE CHANGING FACE OF
FRANCE

Text by VIRGINIA CHANDLER
Photographs by CHRIS FAIRCLOUGH

an imprint of Hodder Children's Books

© White-Thomson Publishing Ltd 2002

Produced for Hodder Wayland by
White-Thomson Publishing Ltd
2/3 St Andrew's Place
Lewes, BN7 1UP

Editor: Alison Cooper
Designer: Christopher Halls at Mind's Eye Design, Lewes
Proofreader: Philippa Smith
Additional picture research: Shelley Noronha, Glass Onion Pictures

First published in Great Britain in 2002 by Hodder Wayland,
an imprint of Hodder Children's Books
Reprinted in 2002

British Library Cataloguing in Publication Data
Chandler, Virginia
   Changing Face of France
   1. France - Juvenile literature I. Title II. France
   944
ISBN 0 7502 3288 9

Printed and bound in Italy by G. Canale & C.S.p.A. Turin

Hodder Children's Books
A division of Hodder Headline Limited
338 Euston Rd, London NW1 3BH

The publisher would like to thank the
following for their contribution: Rob
Bowden – statistics research; Nick Hawken
– statistic panel illustrations; Peter Bull –
map illustration. All photographs are by
Chris Fairclough except: Eye
Ubiquitous/James Davies Travel
Photography 8; Groupe 3A Alliance
Alimentaire 26; Hodder Wayland Picture
Library 17 (top); Impact/Mark Henley 28.

Contents

Toulouse Takes Off

On 9 October 1890, Clément Ader, a carpenter's son from Muret near Toulouse, took off in his flying machine, the *Eole*, and flew for 150 m. *Eole* was the very first aeroplane with an engine and a propeller. It may only have made a short flight, but it was far enough to change the history of the world – and Toulouse. Ader could not have dreamed that his city would one day become one of the world's centres for aviation and aerospace industries.

Toulouse was then a beautiful, historic city, rather isolated from the rest of France and with little industry. Now it is the home of the Concorde and European Airbus passenger planes. The world's largest passenger plane, the A380, will be assembled there. The National Space Research Centre in Toulouse designed the SPOT satellites that photograph the world from space. Private companies have set up there, specializing in telecommunications and satellites, and also in pharmaceuticals and biotechnology.

Toulouse has been transformed. Its busy airport and motorways link it to the rest of France and Europe. It is now the fifth-largest city in France, with the fastest-growing population. One in four people in Toulouse is a student, so the city is lively and dynamic. Clément Ader's sleepy provincial town is really taking off!

▲ *Airbus parts, made in England, Germany, Spain and other parts of France, are assembled in this factory, which is named after Clément Ader.*

▼ *Many old buildings in the centre of Toulouse have been cleaned and renovated. Some of the shopping streets have been pedestrianized.*

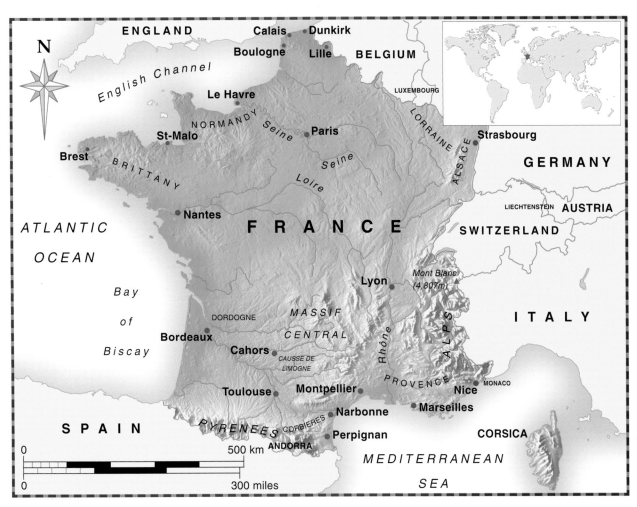

▲ *This map shows the main landscape features and cities of France.*
It also shows many of the places mentioned in this book.

FRANCE: KEY FACTS

Area: 551,000 square km
Population: 58.6 million
Population density: 105 inhabitants per square km
Capital city: Paris (10 million)
Other main cities: Marseilles (1.2 million), Lyon (1.2 million), Lille (1 million), Bordeaux (700,000), Toulouse (700,000), Nice (520,000), Nantes (500,000)
Highest mountain: Mont Blanc (4,807 m)
Longest river: Loire (1,012 km)
Main language: French
Regional languages: Breton, Basque, Occitan, Catalan, Corsican, Alsaçien, Provençal
Religions: Roman Catholic (46 million), Muslim (4 million), Protestant (1 million), Jewish (650,000)
Currency: Euro (1 euro = 100 cents)

2 Past and Present

The French believe that their country has changed more in the last forty years than at any other time in its history. Until 1960, France was a mainly agricultural country. Almost a third of the working population were farmers. They worked on small farms, using traditional methods. Thriving rural villages each had their own shops, businesses and a school. Farms were mostly in the west and south-west, isolated from the rest of the country, whereas important industries were concentrated in the north and east. All the country's financial, political and administrative power centred on Paris, which was the meeting point of all transport links.

▲ *Thirty years ago, a farming scene like this would have been commonplace; today the oxen have been replaced by tractors.*

Decentralization

In 1960, the government decided to modernize France. It also wanted to create a more equal balance between Paris and the rest of France. This process is called decentralization. Over the next fifteen years, huge sums of money were poured into eight cities, to improve and enlarge them and create new jobs. Nine new towns were built, all within close reach of the biggest cities. Many industries and government offices were moved, to spread them more evenly across the country. Science and technology parks were built on the outskirts of a number of university towns, linking research laboratories with cutting-edge, high-tech industries. Farms were enlarged and agriculture was mechanized. In many areas farming has become big business.

Linking new places together

The new or enlarged towns needed new and better transport links. A web of motorways and high-speed railways was built to join the newly developed regions both to Paris and to one another, as well as to neighbouring European countries. The bridges, tunnels and viaducts are superb examples of French engineering skill. Almost 500 million vehicles a year now use the 11,000 kilometres of existing motorways. More motorways are being built or planned to link some of the remoter areas. France is proud of its efficient state-run rail network. Its high-speed train, the TGV, zooms to major cities – Marseilles in the south is now just a three-hour rail journey from Paris.

▲ *Opened in 1995, the Normandy Bridge crosses the River Seine in Normandy, helping to link northern and western France. At 2,141 m, the bridge is one of the longest of its kind in the world.*

IN THEIR OWN WORDS

'My name is Michel Courtois. I joined the CNES, the National Space Research Centre, when it moved from Paris to Toulouse at the end of the 1960s. It was part of the government's plan to make the region a new centre for aerospace and high-tech industries. It was a bit of an adventure moving so far from Paris. Toulouse was a quiet provincial town in those days. But most of the 800 CNES workers agreed to the move. I don't miss Paris at all. We have a much better life here – cheaper housing, easier transport, plenty of sunshine, and the coast and the mountains are just a short drive away!'

The DOM-TOMs

Like several other European countries, France acquired a large empire in the nineteenth century. During the twentieth century, most of its colonies became independent. However, there are still some small territories scattered across the globe that keep close links with France. They are known by the French as the DOM-TOMs (Overseas Departments and Territories). It is politically useful for France to have these territories; for example, France controls the sea and its resources around its territories.

Guiana in South America, the Caribbean islands of Guadeloupe and Martinique, and Réunion in the Indian Ocean have been part of France for over 300 years; they are French overseas departments (DOMs). Their inhabitants speak French, have French nationality, vote in French elections and send their own representatives to Parliament in Paris.

None of these places grows enough food to feed everyone who lives there, and industry is almost non-existent. Tourism is growing and providing a number of jobs, but there is high unemployment. France gives its overseas departments a great deal of financial help so, although they are poor, they are often better off than the neighbouring countries.

French Polynesia, New Caledonia and the Wallis and Futuna Islands in the Pacific Ocean, together with a few small islands in the Antarctic, are French overseas territories (TOMs). In these places, the inhabitants speak their own language and have their own cultural and religious traditions. Local rulers govern alongside the French, not always very happily. Some of these islands may eventually become independent.

▼ *The street market at Pointe-à-Pitre, in Guadeloupe.*

IN THEIR OWN WORDS

'I am Natacha Mai Vinatier. I was born 23 years ago in Martinique, where my French father and Vietnamese mother were teachers. Now I live in Marseilles, studying aid and development – how to bring scientific aid to developing countries. I've just got back from a field trip to Vietnam. A team of students helped the villagers to build an installation to bring drinking water to their homes. We also worked with them on an educational project about the environment and now the villagers we have trained will be able to carry on spreading information about hygiene and pollution. I hope to continue this work in other countries, perhaps in Africa. I have learned so much from working with the villagers, about their way of life and culture. It was a real exchange.'

A world power

Today, France is the world's fifth most important industrial power and tries hard to maintain its political, economic and cultural influence globally. It sends troops to help the United Nations peacekeeping forces in places such as Bosnia and Kosovo. Its humanitarian organization Médecins sans Frontières is known worldwide. France was one of the original six countries that formed the Common Market, which has now expanded to become the European Union. French is spoken as a first or second language in 47 countries. Most of these are in Africa and Asia, and were once ruled by France, but they have now become independent.

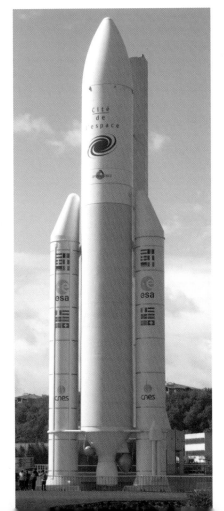

▶ *A scale model of the European satellite launcher, Ariane, at the Toulouse space museum. The French Space Research Centre runs the Ariane programme, and launches the rocket from its base in Guiana, South America.*

3 Landscape and Climate

France is the largest European country after Russia. The French call it 'the Hexagon', because the country fits neatly inside this shape. Three sides are bounded by sea – the English Channel and North Sea to the north, the Atlantic Ocean to the west and the Mediterranean Sea to the south. The other three sides are bordered by land – the Pyrenees mountains in the south-west, the snowy Alps in the south-east, and low-lying country in the north-east. Corsica, an island in the Mediterranean, is also part of France.

▲ Small-scale farms can still be seen in Normandy and Brittany, in the north-west. Their fields are surrounded by trees, hedges or low walls.

The fertile plains

Flat, low-lying plains cover much of north and west France. The Atlantic Ocean influences their climate and these areas have mild winters (with an average temperature of 6 °C in the coldest month) and frequent rainfall – average annual rainfall is 1,126 mm. These conditions are ideal for agriculture.

Traditionally, farming was small scale. Individual farmers grew a variety of cereals and vegetables, tended orchards and kept cows in small fields that surrounded their farmhouses. In some places this way of life still continues. However, over the last fifty years, many small farms have merged to create more efficient mega-farms of more than 300 hectares each.

◄ Farmers have created a mosaic of enormous, open fields for cereal farming, dramatically changing the look of the landscape.

Cereal farming has become more important, and farmers have cut down hedges to make it easier to use huge, modern harvesting machines.

The forests

Trees cover over a quarter of France's land surface (more than anywhere else in Europe apart from Scandinavia), especially in the hilly and mountainous regions that extend towards the east. Here, winters are cold and snowy, and summers are hot and stormy.

Traditional mixed forests are popular places for walks and picnics but most new forest is made up of pine trees. These grow fast and so can be used as timber much sooner than deciduous trees. However, pine forests are dark and gloomy. They shelter few other plants and wildlife, make the soil acidic and attract far fewer visitors.

IN THEIR OWN WORDS

"Arbre mon ami vert, ne pars pas en enfer."

'My name is Robert Paoli. I work for the Mediterranean Forest Protection Agency. In Corsica, where I come from, and in the south of France, the forests are becoming more and more endangered by fire. Thousands of hectares go up in smoke every year. The majority of fires are caused by human carelessness. This poster asks the public to help prevent them. In spring, we clear the forest floor of dead wood and cut corridors to stop any fires from spreading. Then we let sheep or goats graze to keep the ground clear. In the hot, dry summer, staff watch all day long from high towers for signs of smoke, ready to call the firefighters if necessary.'

The high mountains

In the high mountains of the Alps the lowest average temperature is 2 °C and the highest average temperature is 17 °C. Average annual rainfall is 587 mm. Here and in the Pyrenees the soil is too poor, the climate too cold and the growing season too short for mountain farmers to compete with farmers elsewhere. These mountain inhabitants are gradually abandoning their farms.

However, because more and more people have money to spend on holidays, many mountain villages have developed into summer and winter resorts. New hotels, chalets and blocks of flats have been built. In some mountain resorts the buildings have been carefully designed to blend with traditional local building styles. Slopes that were once covered by forest have been cleared for ski runs and ski lifts. This can sometimes expose the villages below to the danger of landslides and avalanches.

▼ *Here, pine forest still covers the lower slopes of the snow-capped Pyrenees.*

IN THEIR OWN WORDS

'I'm Tanguy Gilson. I'm 19 years old and I work in a sports shop in the Pyrenees. In the winter I spend my free time snowboarding, but in the past few years the snow hasn't been very reliable. Some years it comes too late for the Christmas visitors or we get a heavy fall, followed by a thaw. There's talk about global warming and the sport and tourist industries are making new plans for the future. The idea is to show people there is plenty to do in the mountains apart from skiing. We now stock hiking gear, snowshoes and mountain bikes. I'm sure there's still a good future for tourism here. People come all year round to get away from it all, to enjoy the air and the scenery. They'll always be able to count on that.'

The coast

France has over 3,300 km of coastline. The landscape is very varied – chalky cliffs, rocky coves, marshy flatlands and estuaries, shifting sand dunes and lagoons. Some of the coastline has been damaged by natural erosion and pollution or spoilt by too much tourist development. A Coastal Protection Agency now helps to control the effects of tourist and industrial development. It creates protected natural zones and wildlife sanctuaries. It also strictly limits new building.

▲ *The Coastal Protection Agency has bought stretches of the Brittany coast, to preserve it in its wild and natural state.*

The hot south

The south of France is the sunniest part of the country
– it has over 2,500 hours of sunshine per year. In Marseilles,
on the Mediterranean coast, the average maximum
temperature in summer is 23 °C; in winter, the average
temperature of the coldest month is 6 °C. The total average
annual rainfall is 546 mm.

During the summer, the high temperatures and hot winds
can bring drought. Complicated irrigation systems have to be
used to water fruit and vegetable crops, and hedges of tall
cypress trees are used to protect the crops from the wind.
Terraces are cut into the dry, rocky hillsides, and used to
cultivate fruit trees, olive trees and herbs. Although the
winters are mild, violent storms can cause dramatic floods in
spring and autumn. Here, as in other parts of France, these
floods are made worse because roads and car-parks prevent
water from draining away easily, and houses have been built
on river flood plains.

▼ *Fields full of sweet-smelling
lavender, grown for the perfume
industry, are a familiar sight in
southern France.*

Over the last thirty years, the sunny climate has attracted an enormous number of people to move south or go there on holiday. The vast majority of people have moved to towns, such as Nice and Montpellier, which have grown rapidly. Small fishing villages have expanded into huge tourist resorts. New marinas and modern tourist developments have been built along much of the coastline. These cater for over 25 million visitors a year.

▲ *Ideas about tourist development have changed. Densely packed apartments like these on the waterfront at Gruissan would probably not be built today.*

IN THEIR OWN WORDS

'My name is André Daudet. I run a souvenir shop in the marina at Gruissan, near Narbonne on the west Mediterranean coast. It's hard to imagine it now, but thirty years ago there was nothing here but a little fishing village surrounded by salt marshes. My children used to collect shellfish here, just where my shop is now. Then the marshes were drained, and big new resorts and harbours were built all the way down the coast. The marina here is quite pretty, but in my opinion the developers were too greedy – the holiday apartments are too small and packed too closely together. In the summer season it's really overcrowded. I shouldn't really complain. I get plenty of customers, but I still feel sad when I remember how peaceful and beautiful it used to be here.'

4 Natural Resources

France has few natural resources of its own, and so has to import over half of its energy resources as well as most of its minerals. It produces scarcely any oil or gas and its last remaining coal mine will close in 2005.

Energy sources

In the early 1970s, when the price of oil rose very sharply, France decided to develop a nuclear power industry. This provides the country with a cheap source of energy for making electricity. There are now 19 nuclear power stations, which produce so much electricity that France is able to export 15 per cent of it. It also exports its technical skills by supplying engineers to build power stations in other countries. However, France still has to import petrol for cars and lorries.

▲ *Over three-quarters of France's electricity is supplied by nuclear power stations like this one near Dunkirk.*

Hydroelectricity, which used to provide nearly half of France's electricity, now supplies less than 13 per cent of the total. Although it continues to defend its nuclear power policy, France has also started to invest in renewable sources of energy. There is an experimental solar power station in the Pyrenees, a tidal power station in Brittany and wind farms in the north and the south-west.

▶ *By 2005, the French state electricity company plans to have between 500 and 1,000 wind turbines producing between 250 and 500 megawatts of electricity.*

IN THEIR OWN WORDS

'My name is Dominique Deschamps, I'm a geography teacher, and an active member of an ecology organization. There has always been much less criticism of nuclear power in France than in other countries – it has been accepted as a way of keeping the country independent in terms of energy, and of supplying fairly cheap electricity. But some people, particularly the young, are becoming more aware of the possible hazards. There is growing interest in renewable energies. Hydroelectric power has long been an important source of electricity but building the mountain dams is so expensive. EDF, the state electricity company, is developing the use of wind farms, but we still lag far behind countries like Germany or Denmark. Household waste that cannot be recycled is starting to be converted into energy too: electricity, heat or gases used in industry. France is the leading producer of renewable energies in the EU, but as I tell my pupils, we still have a very long way to go.'

Forestry

France's forests provide timber for buildings and furniture, and wood pulp for papermaking. Although the size of forested areas doubled in the twentieth century, France still does not produce enough timber to meet all its needs. Two severe hurricanes in 1999 destroyed millions of trees in France's forests. Some regions lost ten years' worth of production. It will be a hundred years before the forests are restored.

◀ *A sawmill near Cahors, where logs are cut up for use in the timber industry.*

Agriculture

France's most important natural resource is its farmland. The French call it their 'green oil'. The cool, damp climate and good-quality soil that covers over half the country enable France to produce more food than it needs to feed its own population. Surplus food is exported, and, after the USA, France is the largest exporter of food in the world. The main exports are wheat, milk and milk products (such as cheese, yoghurt and butter), and sugar beet.

▲ *This sheep farmer raises sheep for both meat and milk. The milk is used to make the famous Roquefort blue cheese.*

Wine production

Wine is one of France's most important products, both at home and as an export. Some vineyards used to produce rough, everyday wine; others produced famous wines, bought the world over. In recent years, the French have been drinking less, but better tasting, wine. French wine exports have to compete with the ever-increasing amount of wine produced by other countries.

Many winegrowers have had to make a choice – either to leave their vineyards as they are and earn less and less, or to modernize and produce better wine. This often involves borrowing huge sums of money from banks. However, modernizing is more likely to give the winegrowers a better income in the future. Younger winegrowers are often more prepared to take the risk, while older winegrowers or those who cannot borrow enough money have tended not to modernize.

IN THEIR OWN WORDS

'My name is Louis Fabre. I'm a wine grower in the Corbières, near the western Mediterranean. I produce 17 different wines from 300 hectares of land. About a third of the wine is organic, from vines treated only with natural fertilizers and insecticides. But, in fact, for all our wines, we use methods that respect the soil and the environment, and spray only when we need to. For many years, this region was known for mass-produced, cheap, rough wines. Things are changing, and now we prefer to make smaller quantities of better-quality wines. My family has been making wine here for fourteen generations. I want to hand on to my children vineyards that will be healthy and in harmony with nature for years to come.'

Modernizing the vineyards

Modernizing a vineyard involves replanting it with new vines that produce better wine, and planting the vines further apart, so that the grapes can be harvested by machine. It takes time for the new vines to grow. The winegrower has to wait for around seven years before the first grapes can be harvested.

▶ *These vineyards are in the Corbières region.*

Sea change

With shores facing the North Sea, the English Channel, the Atlantic and the Mediterranean, France has a long tradition of both coastal and deep-sea fishing. But fishing is now in crisis. Over-fishing has reduced the stocks of fish in the seas and strict regulations have been introduced to limit how much fishermen are allowed to catch. Competition from other European countries, Spain in particular, has lowered fish prices. People are eating less fish than before, and often prefer to buy frozen fish, which may come from distant parts of the world.

Fewer fishermen

Small fishing boats still land daily catches in Brittany, on the west coast. Industrial fleets of big ships, with deep-freeze facilities and radar for tracking shoals, net huge tonnages of fish. They bring them back to large ports, such as Boulogne, which have modernized their unloading and storage facilities. However, France has only 10,000 fishermen today, half the number there were in the early 1990s. This high-risk, dangerous and demanding job does not appeal to many young people and investing in modern fishing boats is very expensive.

▼ *Most fishermen use trawlers like these, going out into the North Sea, or the European waters of the Atlantic.*

IN THEIR OWN WORDS

'My name is Alain Fontaine. I'm a fisherman in the port of Erquy, near St Malo, in Brittany. I mostly fish for crabs and scallops, and sell my catch directly to the restaurants in nearby tourist resorts. A lot of fishing here is from small boats like mine. It's expensive to equip a boat for deep-sea fishing. The big worry for me is pollution. Two tankers have been wrecked off the coast recently, spilling oil and chemicals into the sea. We had to stop selling our shellfish until they had passed strict controls. My father and grandfather taught me all I know and I always wanted to follow on from them. But it's a hard way to make a living and dangerous too. My younger brother has left the sea. He's gone to work at the Citroën car factory in Rennes.'

Farming the sea

Along parts of the Atlantic coast and the western Mediterranean the sea is shallow and there is a mixture of fresh and salt water in the estuaries. These are ideal conditions for oyster and mussel farming, which is flourishing. However, shellfish are at risk from pollution, disease and extreme weather. Many oyster beds were badly affected by oil spills and the damaging hurricane of 1999.

▶ *In France there are 50,000 'farmers of the sea', raising oysters, mussels and other shellfish. They often sell direct to customers to make more profit.*

5

The Changing Environment

The changing towns

Today, over three-quarters of French people live in towns or cities, but most of them do not live in town centres. They may live in new towns some distance from the city where they work, or in the thousands of new suburban houses that have been built on land once used for farming. Many more live in huge, high-rise estates that ring the outskirts of large towns. Some of these estates, built quickly in the 1960s and 1970s to house workers in the new industries, have aged badly. They have become pockets of poverty and social problems.

▲ *High-rise housing in Belleville, on the outskirts of Paris. Many estates built in the 1960s are becoming run down, so some tower blocks are being demolished.*

IN THEIR OWN WORDS

'I'm Mohamed Bouchiki. I'm 12 years old. My family moved to France from Algeria ten years ago. We live in a big housing estate outside Toulouse. Some of the other estates have a bad name because of crime or violence, but I'm happy here. The youth workers here do a lot for the kids. They run a club to help anyone who has problems at school or at home, or who gets into trouble. And they organize activities after school – there was a hip-hop workshop in the last holidays. I'm in the football club. Sport is important because it teaches you to respect the rules and to respect one another. I'd like to be a professional footballer when I grow up. My hero is Zinedine Zidane.'

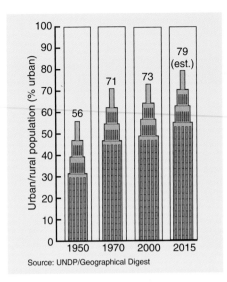

Later developers learnt from the early planning mistakes. More care was taken to provide shops, schools and leisure facilities on the estates, and to group smaller blocks of flats more attractively. New housing schemes now have to include a certain number of low-rent, subsidized homes so that low-income families have a better choice of places to live.

New schools, hospitals and shopping centres have been built for the growing numbers of townspeople. Improved transport – motorways, ring roads and suburban rail lines – link the suburbs and outskirts with the town centres.

Many historic centres have been cleaned and renovated. Their streets are lined with smart shops, galleries and restaurants. Old industrial buildings or warehouses have been replaced by luxury apartments or modern offices. Increasingly, town centres are being pedestrianized or have introduced trams, bicycle and bus lanes, and underground railways. This makes them more attractive and less polluted or congested by traffic.

Source: UNDP/Geographical Digest

▲ *It is estimated that almost 80 per cent of the French population will live in towns and cities by 2015.*

◄ *New hypermarkets and superstores have been built outside towns, often on ring roads. People need cars to reach them.*

Paris – the changing capital

Paris is like a magnet. In spite of all attempts to decentralize, it continues to attract people, particularly the young and the highly educated. Almost 20 per cent of the French population live in and around Paris – an area that makes up just 2 per cent of the whole country! The city is seven times larger than Marseilles, its nearest rival, and greater Paris has more people than the whole of either Belgium or Portugal.

Although people still want to live and work in the capital, fewer people now live in central Paris than in the past. As the roads and railways improve, it has become possible for more and more people to live in the suburbs, where housing is cheaper. The suburbs now have four times the population of the city itself.

Millions of people travel for well over an hour, some from towns as far as 100 kilometres away, to work in or near Paris. Over half of the commuters travel by car, so there are traffic jams every morning and evening, and the level of air pollution is worsening. The rest travel by the fast cross-Paris train (RER), the underground (Metro) or suburban trains.

▲ *Though built at the start of the twentieth century, the Metro is very efficient and cheap. It carries 4.5 million people a day.*

◄ *Although the city has good public transport systems, many Parisians prefer to travel by car. The result is traffic jams and pollution.*

Paris is very much the powerhouse of the country, and not just because it is the seat of government. It is still the centre of finance, home to the Stock Exchange and the headquarters of virtually every bank. Most of the head offices of France's 500 major firms are based there. Over a quarter of French students study at its many universities. Internationally-known fashion houses and the manufacturers of luxury goods have their showrooms in the heart of the city. In addition, Paris is the most-visited tourist destination in the world, with dozens of museums, art galleries and many other forms of entertainment.

▶ *La Défense, a futuristic business complex, provides offices for 140,000 Parisians.*

IN THEIR OWN WORDS

'My name is Jean-Paul Leclerc. I work in the traffic division of the Paris police. Directing traffic here is quite a high-risk job! Parisian drivers have a bad reputation – very often they do not respect pedestrians or cyclists, though there are new bicycle lanes in the city now, and on Sundays the roads along the River Seine are shut to cars, so that walkers and roller-skaters can enjoy the city. One of the main problems with all these cars is the pollution they cause. There is now a partial ban on cars when pollution levels go above a certain level, but this is difficult for us to enforce. Commuters should make more effort to share cars for their journeys to work – it would save them money, and help reduce traffic jams as well.'

Changes in farming

Farms are far larger and fewer today than they were in the past. Farmers use huge tractors and expensive, specialized machinery for sowing, spraying and harvesting crops, such as wheat, sunflowers, beet and other vegetables. There is even a customized vacuum cleaner for harvesting lettuces. Big farms employ few workers and use artificial fertilizers and pesticides to produce as many crops as possible.

In Brittany during the 1950s and 1960s, many farmers changed from growing vegetables to intensive farming of pigs, cows and battery hens. Farmers ran up huge debts setting up such farms, but the farms did prove to be very efficient. The problem was that so much meat and so many eggs were produced that the price farmers could get for their produce fell dramatically. Now many farmers rely on financial support from the European Union to stay in business.

Farmers have tried different techniques to increase production. For example, they used to give hormones to calves to make them grow faster although this has now been banned. Experiments have started on genetically

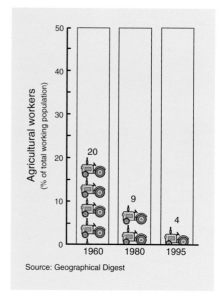

Source: Geographical Digest

▲ *Notice how steeply the number of farm workers has fallen in the last 40 years.*

◀ *The food-processing industry is one of the most important in France and it exports its products worldwide. This is the control room of a milk-processing plant.*

modified (GM) crops, which are said to be more resistant to disease. But since the 1990s there have been a number of food scares connected to intensive farming. Diseases such as BSE in cattle have been passed on to humans. Many people have become alarmed by the problems linked to agribusiness.

People are also concerned about pollution from large-scale farming. Chemicals sprayed on to the fields and the waste produced by animals reared intensively are polluting water supplies. Fertile topsoil is washed away by the rain or blown by the wind from fields that now have few hedges to help keep the soil in place.

▲ *The use of agricultural chemicals for spraying against pests has multiplied sixfold in the last thirty years.*

IN THEIR OWN WORDS

'I am Pascal Gamas, a scientist working at one of the state agriculture research laboratories. We are trying to find ways to improve the agriculture of tomorrow. Here, for example, we are studying the way that bacteria in the soil can help plants grow. Our research will help produce plants that can resist diseases and pests, and that can grow well in different soils and climates. We work on natural ways to enrich the soil. The aim is to cut back the use of artificial fertilizers that pollute the soil and water. The farming of the future must respect the environment and feed a growing population with high-yield, healthy produce.'

Better food

Frightened by the food scares, people are increasingly willing to pay more to make sure they eat safer and tastier food. Public demand is encouraging more farmers to grow organic fruit and vegetables. The BSE crisis has prompted cattle farmers to grow their own winter feed, instead of relying on supplies from huge industrial feed companies. Open-air pig farms are multiplying. These produce better-quality pork.

Some farmers have formed associations to promote varieties of apples, plums and other fruits that are in danger of dying out. They hold annual fruit fairs so the public can taste and learn about different varieties, and buy saplings to grow in their gardens at home.

▲ These cattle are fed on fodder crops grown by the farmer. It is spring, and the grass is not yet growing fast enough for grazing.

◄ A market stall in Brittany selling organic fruit and vegetables. Organic food production is one of the fastest-growing areas of agriculture.

Small specialist farmers are growing in number. They prosper by concentrating on regional specialities, including cheeses, cured hams and sausages (*charcuterie*). Some farmers raise rare breeds of animal, such as angora rabbits or ostriches. Others produce expensive luxury foods, such as *foie gras* (duck liver pâté).

Changes in country life

The massive expansion of towns and the revolution in farming over the last fifty years have drastically changed country life. Every year, people in remote and isolated country villages leave their homes for good. Young people leave because they cannot find suitable work locally. Many children of farmers do not want to take over the family farm when they grow up. They prefer to find easier and better-paid work in towns.

▶ *Many small farms in the south-west raise geese or ducks to make* foie gras, *the much-prized liver pâté.*

GODARD

SPÉCIALISTE DU FOIE GRAS

IN THEIR OWN WORDS

'My name is Gerard Cavaillé. I own a small farm up on the plateau of the Causse de Limogne in south-west France. I never married – a lot of farmers round here are single as it's a lonely life here for women – so I've no son to take over from me. Anyway, young people are not interested in farming this land. The soil is stony and the climate can be harsh. They've all moved away to work in the towns. Back in the 1950s, every village on the Causse had a shop and a school. There were thirty farms, each with a dairy herd, a few pigs and some fields of mixed crops. But it's a hard way to make a living. Now there are only two farms left, and the shops and schools have closed.'

The empty diagonal

A huge sweep of under-populated countryside now runs from the Belgian border in the north-east through the centre of France to the Pyrenees in the south-west. The French call this 'the empty diagonal'. In these areas, the average age of the population is much older than elsewhere, people's incomes are lower, big towns are few and far between and transport links are poor.

Hope for the country

There is new life in some isolated areas. The creation of regional nature reserves attracts thousands of tourists, who come to walk, canoe, fish, climb or observe wildlife. Local farmers can earn extra income from feeding and lodging these 'green tourists' and the protected areas safeguard the landscape and wildlife for the future.

In some parts of France, English, Dutch and Belgian families, as well as some French people, have bought abandoned farm buildings cheaply and converted them into second homes. The most popular areas for second homes

▲ *This abandoned farm in the Causse de Limogne may find a new life as a second home.*

◀ *Picturesque hill villages like this one near Perpignan in the Pyrenees attract plenty of visitors during the tourist season but are lonely places to live in during the winter.*

have been the Alps, the Dordogne, and Provence in the south. A campaign was recently launched to persuade more city-dwellers to buy houses in the more remote rural areas where falling populations are a serious problem.

Commuter villages

Some country communities near large cities, such as Paris, Lyon and Montpellier, have grown in recent years. They have become commuter villages, home to city workers who prefer to live in the green space and cleaner air of the countryside. As telecommunications improve, more people may be able to work from home, using the internet to communicate with colleagues and customers. The internet is also helping to prevent rural schools with only a few pupils from being closed down. Teachers use the computer network to link up with teachers and pupils in other areas. Older pupils still have to travel long distances to their nearest secondary school but younger pupils can go to their village school. This may also help to bring new life to France's villages.

IN THEIR OWN WORDS

'Hello! We're Melissa, Laure, Loïc and Olivier. We're aged between 9 and 11. In our little village school there's just one class, with 25 pupils and one teacher. We have three computers and we use the software or the internet every day to help us with our work. We've even made our own website. It tells you all about our village and our activities. Last month we went on a caving trip and we wrote about that. We put games and quizzes on the site too, and people from all over the world can join us. We live a long way from a town but we've worked on projects with classes in Norway, the USA and Japan – we've got the world in our classroom! Come and visit us on our website! (www2.ac-toulouse.fr/piquecos//piquecos.html)'

The Changing Population

6

Between the end of the Second World War in 1945 and the 1960s there was a 'baby boom', when the population grew from 40 million to 50 million. Since the 1960s people have been having fewer babies. They are able to plan their families and may choose to have fewer children because more mothers want to go out to work, or because they cannot afford a large family.

On the other hand, people are living longer. France has an excellent health service, with high numbers of doctors and specialists, and modern, well-equipped hospitals. As a result of high-quality health care and improvements in diet and hygiene, men can now expect to live to 73 years, and women to 82.

An ageing population

Fewer babies, longer lives – this means that the population is gradually ageing. In the twenty-first century, an increasing percentage will be retired and elderly. Many old people live in the country, where there are fewer doctors and hospitals. Often, they face problems of loneliness because their children and neighbours have moved away to live in the towns.

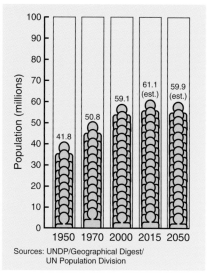

Sources: UNDP/Geographical Digest/ UN Population Division

▲ *France's population grew by almost 50 per cent in the second half of the twentieth century but is expected to remain almost static over the next fifty years.*

◀ *Improved medical care means that France's population can look forward to a long and healthy retirement. These elderly men are enjoying a favourite leisure activity, playing a game of boules.*

IN THEIR OWN WORDS

'I'm Nadia Amokrane, I'm 35 years old and I'm a youth worker. My parents came to France in 1963, with the first wave of immigrants from Algeria. My three brothers and I were born here. We always spoke French at home, but in the long summer holidays back in Algeria we learnt Kabyl. Algeria seemed a strange and wonderful place to me! My parents brought me up in the strict Muslim way, but when I was 18, I rebelled. I wanted to live my life like the other French girls of my age. It was a hard time for us all. Now I feel I can keep the two parts of me – I am building my life here in France but I love my Algerian culture, the music and the food. I don't want to lose it, I want to pass it on to my own little girl. It's not easy. France is a multicultural society, but it doesn't want to admit it!'

Changing faces

Many immigrants from France's former colonies, especially Algeria, came to work in France in the 1960s. Today, the children of those immigrants are grown-up and have families of their own. Most have French nationality and feel that they are as French as anyone else. Some find, however, that it is hard to make a place in society, and have more difficulty in finding jobs or housing. They see that there are few people from ethnic minorities on TV or in politics.

Young people have reacted by creating their own culture. The city housing estates produce talented artists in street fashion, dance, rap music and sport. France has traditionally preferred its immigrants to blend in and adopt its lifestyle. But perhaps this too will change, and it will start to admit that they have something special and valuable to contribute.

▼ *Football clubs run by youth workers attract young people from all communities in the city housing estates.*

7

Changes at Home

The family is important to the French, but their families are changing. Compared with their parents, young people are marrying later. (The average age for men to marry is 28 and for women it is 26.) Couples may marry after they have a child together, or decide not to marry at all (a third of all babies are born to unmarried couples). Families are also smaller than they were in the years after the Second World War, when the government encouraged people to have large families and gave them extra financial help. Divorced and single-parent families are on the increase.

Rising incomes

In the last fifty years, incomes have trebled. Many families live in comfortable, often modern, homes with central heating and bathrooms – whereas in 1954, 90 per cent of homes had no bath or shower. The majority can afford to buy a car and household equipment such as a television, a fridge-freezer, a washing machine and a hi-fi. Almost half of all homes have two televisions.

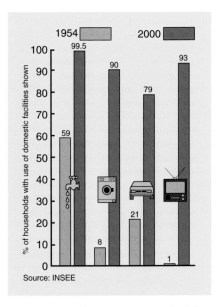

Source: INSEE

▲ Almost all French households are now equipped with electrical goods such as TVs and washing machines.

◄ Both of Benoît Couillet's parents go out to work and his family has a good standard of living. Benoît has a synthesizer and a computer in his bedroom.

The poor

By contrast, an estimated 5 million people in France live in poverty. This may be because they are jobless, or their families have broken down, or because they earn only the minimum wage. Over 2 million of them have no permanent address or are completely homeless. Almost all of the homeless live either in or just outside big cities, mainly in the Paris area, the east (where traditional industries are in decline) and the Mediterranean region.

Everyone, however poor, can get health care and education from the state, and most can claim welfare payments to help them get by. Charities provide meals, clothing or shelter. But poverty is hard to bear in a society where most people can afford comfortable homes and have money to spend on the latest consumer goods. There is a great divide between the haves and have-nots.

▲ *Many people now have more leisure time and more money to spend on consumer goods, so shopping malls like this one near Calais are increasingly popular.*

IN THEIR OWN WORDS

'I'm Benoît Sauquet and I'm 25 years old. I'm a social work graduate and I help to run a charity grocery shop. Our customers are people in difficulty – the unemployed, the homeless, people on benefit or asylum seekers. They are sent to us by the social services, and they can buy what they need in the shop for just 10 per cent of the normal price. We give them advice too if they want it, for example about how to plan a healthy diet or how to prepare food. We have about 40 customers a day. Our stock is mostly surplus goods donated by supermarkets, farmers or the European Union. It makes me angry to see these big shopping centres pushing people to spend more and more. Those who can't, like my clients, feel shut out of society.'

Changes in leisure

People work fewer hours than ever before. Most employees work, on average, between 35 and 39 hours a week, and have five weeks' paid holiday per year. A great many young people are staying in education for longer and so are starting their working lives later. Many older people are retiring early. This means that people of all ages have more free time to enjoy other activities.

The French have more holidays than any other country in Europe. Most people go away at least once a year, usually in the summer. The great majority stay in France. There is a trend away from relaxing beach holidays and towards more active country holidays, such as walking or doing sport.

▲ *The wide, windy beaches of northern France are ideal for sand-yachting.*

◄ *Paris is famous for its pavement cafés; today internet cafés are springing up around the city.*

IN THEIR OWN WORDS

'My name is Cécile Manent and I'm 18 years old. I'm a student at a hotel and catering school and my ambition is to be a pastry chef. Although half the students here are girls, there are not many women chefs – I'm hoping to help change that! My parents used to run a restaurant, so I've been cooking and enjoying fine food since I was little. Fast-food places are all right for a snack, but when my friends and I want an evening out we go to a good restaurant. We are all sure to find good jobs when we leave because there's a big demand for well-trained specialists. French cooking still has a great future. There have been so many food scares, and I think the public is turning back to traditional dishes using local, high-quality produce.'

Changes in diet

French cooking has long been considered to be amongst the best in the world. Traditionally, French family meals were based on local produce, bought in markets and freshly cooked at home. Now people can visit the local supermarket and buy food from all over the world. They often choose ready-made dishes and frozen foods, which can be cooked quickly. The number of fast-food restaurants and snack-bars is increasing, whereas the number of traditional restaurants is declining. Thirty years ago, there were 200,000 restaurants; now there are only 80,000.

Food is less rich than it was in the past and people spend less time over their meals. It is becoming less common for families to eat together. However, in general, the French of all ages (if they can afford it) are interested and concerned about eating quality food. They are knowledgeable shoppers. In most towns, people can still buy fresh produce at a market.

8

Changes at Work

Compared with the past, there are few jobs which people can now expect to do for life. Some jobs have disappeared altogether. The use of robots in car factories and increased mechanization in many other factories mean that they need fewer workers. Small, specialist shopkeepers, such as ironmongers, grocers and shoe-menders, are closing down both in the town centres and in the country. They cannot compete with the low prices, variety and convenience of out-of-town superstores. On the other hand, there are more and more new jobs that did not exist before, in the computer industry, fast-food restaurants, internet cafés or mobile phone shops for example.

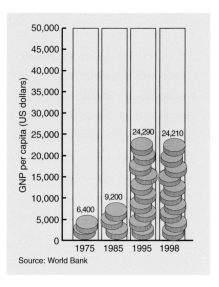

Source: World Bank

▲ *The value of the goods and services France produces is almost four times greater today than in 1975.*

Industries in decline

Since the 1970s many traditional industries have declined, whilst new high-tech ones are flourishing. The north and east

IN THEIR OWN WORDS

'I'm Valérie Hibon. I work in a fast-food restaurant in this huge new shopping centre just outside Calais in Coquelles, near the Channel Tunnel terminus. The tunnel, the high-speed trains and the new motorways have made a big difference to this area. It's become a shoppers' paradise. We get visitors from Britain, Belgium and even the Netherlands. Some of them come on just a day trip to stock up on French food, wine and clothes. There's been a lot of unemployment in the north. My dad lost his job when they closed the shipyards in Dunkirk. But shopping centres like this have brought new jobs for local people, and new hope for the future.'

▲ *A cargo ship unloading in the docks at Dunkirk.*

were once the homes of 'heavy' industries, such as coal and iron mining, steel making, textiles and shipbuilding. The coal and iron mines have closed, either because there was no coal or iron ore left to mine or because they no longer made enough money. The steel, textile and ship-building industries have declined because the products they made were being produced more cheaply by competitors in the Far East. Factories were abandoned and the area became an industrial wasteland. The ports suffered too, since fewer goods were being exported. Unemployment in these industrial areas rose far above the national average.

Some new industries, such as car factories and mail-order firms, have opened in the north, where there are good, new transport links. Several old industries have specialized in order to stay in business. One shipyard, for example, specializes in making pleasure boats. Some textile companies make high-tech industrial fabrics for use in buildings and road construction.

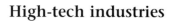
High-tech industries

High-tech industries, such as those making trains, aeroplanes and space satellites, are booming and have become world famous. The French have exported their high-speed trains (TGVs), for example, to places as far afield as Korea and Florida, USA. The car industry is still important. Other successful industries produce pharmaceuticals, petrochemicals, electrical and electronic equipment, and luxury goods (companies making luxury goods employ 200,000 people).

The new industries are spread around France, often in areas where, previously, there were very few. The car factories of Citroën, Peugeot and Renault are dotted across the top half of the country. High-tech industries are scattered throughout France, near large towns with universities and research institutes.

▶ *The tiny two-seater Smart car, made in Lorraine in eastern France, is one of the latest creations of the car industry.*

IN THEIR OWN WORDS

'My name is Fabienne Rougeot. I'm 20 years old and I'm an engineering student at the National School of Aeronautics and Space. Ever since I was little I've been fascinated by space and the planets. My dream is to work on the space travel programmes, or even to design a space station on Mars! Only one in ten students here is a girl, but I'm not worried about working in a male-dominated field. I think attitudes have changed. You are judged by what you can do, not by your sex. There's a great future for young engineers in the French aviation and aerospace industries. Progress is being made all the time – look at the giant new Airbus 380, for example, it may mean hundreds of new jobs. And who knows how much there is to discover out there in space!'

IN THEIR OWN WORDS

'My name is Elizabeth Crouzet. I work in a baker's shop. We have recently had to get used to a very big change at work – the switch from the franc to the new euro currency. I was very worried because we didn't have any training to help us deal with it. The worst time was between 1 January 2002, when the euro was introduced, and 18 February, when the old franc disappeared. During that time people could pay for their bread in francs, but we had to give them their change in euros. You can imagine the muddle! Some people kept two purses, one for francs, one for euros. We have a special cash register that shows the price in both currencies, but some people still thought we'd pushed the prices up. Although most people have accepted the change, the elderly are still confused and I think some will never get used to it.'

Service industries

As the number of workers in farming and industry has fallen, the number in service and communications jobs has increased. Three million service jobs have been created since 1970. Now, nearly 70 per cent of French workers are employed in business, shops, transport, health, education, tourism, finance, insurance or administration. Over two-and-a-half million people are employed by the state.

The service sector is growing to meet increasing demands at home. But it is also important abroad, where French companies have set up hotels, banks, tourist centres and stores. You can now find a French hypermarket in Brazil, a catering school in Japan and a luxury hotel in Lebanon.

Working women

These days nearly as many women work outside the home as men. Women are better qualified than in the past. Fifty years ago far fewer girls than boys passed the school-leaving exam or went to university, but girls have now overtaken the boys. Working mothers are helped by good childcare – most three-year-olds can find a place in the state nursery schools.

However, most women still do not earn as much as men. On average, they earn 27 per cent less. This may be because it is easier for them to find work in low-paid jobs, or because over a quarter of them only do paid work part-time. Such jobs make it easier to fit in running a home, still mostly a woman's task, but they tend to pay less well. Also, women often find it harder to reach senior positions at work – very few women hold important posts in business or industry, and France has one of the lowest numbers of women politicians in Europe. There is still some male prejudice against women in positions of power. In 2001, a law made political parties put forward equal numbers of men and women candidates in local elections. But in the workplace, it is up to the younger, more equal-minded generation to change old attitudes.

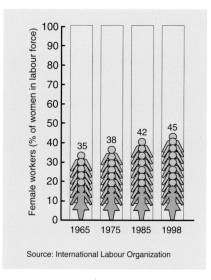

Source: International Labour Organization

▲ *Women now make up just under half the total workforce.*

Foreign workers

France has a long tradition of welcoming foreign workers, many of them from former colonies in Africa and Asia. From the 1960s, large numbers of Italians, Spanish and Portuguese came to work in agriculture, and industrial workers came from the Maghreb (Algeria, Tunisia and Morocco). Since the 1980s and 1990s, smaller numbers of workers have come from the West African countries of Senegal and Mali, and also from Turkey, China and Vietnam.

▶ *Many jobs that were once held only by men are now done by women too: Rose-Marie Ferrer, shown here, is a bus driver.*

Creating new jobs

The French economy entered a crisis at the end of the 1980s. Unemployment nearly doubled between 1988 and 1993, rising from 1.8 million to 3 million. Immigrants were the first to be hit by the sudden rise in unemployment. Young people were also badly affected, with a quarter of those aged 16–25 unemployed in the depth of the recession.

The government introduced two measures to create more jobs. They gave young people 'youth jobs' in schools, the police and local government offices. They also reduced official working hours from 40 to 35 hours a week. The aim of this was to encourage employers to take on extra workers.

▲ *Many young people do short-term or part-time jobs, such as delivering pizzas.*

IN THEIR OWN WORDS

'I'm Chrystel Krakenberger, from Alsace in eastern France. I'm 24 years old and I have a job with the Youth Employment Scheme, working in a secondary school. I help the children with their homework, give extra coaching and keep order in the playground. In my spare time, I'm preparing for my exams to qualify as a science teacher. There's a lot of competition – only 800 are successful each year out of 4,000 applicants. Teaching is popular, partly because working for the state means job security and a good pension. But I love working with children and helping them to learn. My job here has proved that to me. My mother and two sisters are teachers too, so it runs in the family.'

9

The Way Ahead

When a magazine survey asked foreigners what they thought was the main fault of the French, the answer was, 'They are very pleased with themselves'. Perhaps at the start of the new century the French have a lot to be pleased about. Their economic crisis seems to be behind them. France is a leading country in agriculture, exports and tourism. Its food, art and culture are admired, and envied, the world over.

But, at the same time, the French are anxious. Too many people are still excluded from the general prosperity. The beauty of their towns and countryside is at risk from pollution and over-development. Even their language and culture seem threatened – English pop songs, American films and fast-food restaurants are everywhere.

◄ France is benefiting from improved transport links, such as the high-speed trains bringing passengers from London to the Gare du Nord station in the heart of Paris.

IN THEIR OWN WORDS

'My name is Katia Lengrand and I'm 25 years old. I'm a tourist guide, and I also teach tourism students. France is the most-visited country in the world – the tourist industry employs over 2 million people and is very important to the economy. I believe holidaymakers want to do more than just sit on a beach in the sun. They want to explore the countryside, learn about art or history, discover a new sport. I love helping people find out just how much France has to offer. We have a very rich past but this is a modern country too, not just a big museum. For me, the old and new go together. We should conserve our culture and traditions but use the new technologies – high-speed transport and the internet – to bring them to people. This is the way forward.'

The French wish to enjoy all the benefits of the modern world. They want to play an active part in the Europe and the world of tomorrow. Nonetheless, young and old are also keen to preserve a quality of life that has its roots in tradition, and a way of doing and seeing things that they speak of as 'the French difference'. This may be a difficult balancing act in a changing society, but France is determined to take the best of its past into the future.

◀ *The Louvre, the world-famous art museum in Paris, combines the old and the new. The modern underground entrance to the restored, old, stone buildings is topped by a futuristic glass pyramid.*

Glossary

Aerospace industries Industries producing spacecraft, rockets and missiles.

Agribusiness Large-scale, industrial farming and food-processing, often controlled by a large company rather than an individual farmer.

Agriculture Farming.

Asylum seekers People who have left their home countries because they do not feel safe and have asked the authorities in a different country for permission to live there instead.

Avalanche A fast-moving fall of snow, ice and rock down a mountainside.

Aviation industries Industries involved in the design and production of aircraft.

Biotechnology Using micro-organisms to carry out processes that are useful to human beings, such as processing waste materials.

BSE Bovine Spongiform Encephalopathy, a disease that began to affect cattle in the late twentieth century, and can be passed on to humans if they eat infected beef.

Colonies Countries that are ruled by another country.

Commuter A worker, living in the suburbs or the country, who travels daily to a city office.

Consumer goods Goods that people use in their everyday lives, such as TVs or fridges.

Decentralization The outward movement of people, jobs and services from an area where these are concentrated.

Drought A long period of time when there is little or no rainfall.

Economy The entire wealth-creating activity of a country.

European Union (EU) A group of countries in Europe that work together to strengthen the economic and political links between them. Some of the member countries share the same currency, the euro.

Exports Goods sold by one country to others.

Fertilizers Substances mixed into the soil to enrich it and help crops to grow.

Global warming An increase in temperatures around the world, which many scientists believe is caused by pollution in the atmosphere.

GNP Gross National Product, the total value of goods and services produced by a country in one year. This figure is divided by the number of the total population to work out the amount produced by each person ('per capita' is Latin and means 'per person').

Hormones Chemicals that occur naturally in the body. Some can also be produced artificially and given to animals, for example, to speed up natural processes such as growth.

Hurricane An extremely violent wind.

Hydroelectricity Electricity generated by using the power of falling water to turn turbines.

Hypermarket A self-service store, which is larger and sells a wider range of goods than a supermarket.

Immigrants People who have left one country and come to live in another.

Income The money that people receive for their work or from their investments.

Independent A country that is free to govern itself, instead of being ruled by another country.

Irrigation Watering the land artificially, using, for example, channels or sprinklers.

Organic farming A way of farming that does not use artificial fertilizers or pesticides.

Pedestrianized Streets converted for use only by people on foot, instead of by traffic.

Pesticides Substances that farmers and gardeners use to kill insects that damage their crops.

Petrochemicals Substances obtained from petroleum and used in industry.

Pharmaceuticals Medical drugs.

Provincial All parts of a country outside the capital city.

Recession A period when businesses are not doing well and unemployment rises.

Renewable energy Energy from sources that will not run out, such as the wind, the tides and the sun.

Rural Countryside.

Science park A place where there is a large number of scientific institutes and high-tech companies.

Service jobs Jobs in shops, tourism or banking, etc., where workers are providing a service rather producing goods.

Suburb A district joined to a town, usually mainly residential (that is, where people live).

Urban Of or belonging to a city or town.

Further Information

Books

Country Studies: France by Celia Tidmarsh (Heinemann, 1999)

A Flavour of France by Teresa Fisher (Wayland, 1998)

France File: Facts about France (in French) edited by Simon Thorp (Carel Press, 1996)

Montreuil: A European Place Study co-ordinated by Don Garman (Geographical Association, 1995)

Country Insights: France by Teresa Fisher (Wayland, 1996)

Country Fact Files: France by Véronique Bussolin (Macdonald Young Books, 1997)

Websites

www.Francetreasures.com

A guide to the landscape and history of France, with advice on places of interest.

www.zipzapfrance.com

A young person's guide to France and its way of life produced in French and English.

www.francetourism.com

The official website for the French government tourist office in the United States, which also provides information about French territories in the Caribbean such as Martinique.

www.pitt.edu/~wwwes/france.nhp.html

A 'virtual library' of French studies, produced by the University of Pittsburgh in the USA and suitable for older readers and teachers.

www.louvre.fr

A guide to the world-famous Louvre museum in Paris.

www.franceguide.com

The website of the French Government Tourist Office in the UK

www.discoverfrance.net

A wide-ranging site covering many aspects of French life.

Useful addresses

French Government Tourist Office
278 Piccadilly, London WIJ 0AL
Tel: 0906 8244123

Index

Page numbers in **bold** refer to photographs, maps or statistics panels.